TEN

TEN
NEW POETS

EDITED BY
**BERNARDINE EVARISTO
& DALJIT NAGRA**

spread the word

BLOODAXE BOOKS

Introduction copyright © Bernardine Evaristo 2010
Poems copyright © contributors as listed 2010

ISBN: 978 1 85224 879 6

First published 2010 by
Spread the Word,
77 Lambeth Walk,
London SE11 6DX,
in association with
Bloodaxe Books Ltd,
Highgreen,
Tarset,
Northumberland NE48 1RP.

www.bloodaxebooks.com
For further information about Bloodaxe titles
please visit our website or write to
the above address for a catalogue.

Supported by
**ARTS COUNCIL
ENGLAND**

Cover design: Neil Astley & Pamela Robertson-Pearce.

Printed in Great Britain by
Bell & Bain Limited, Glasgow, Scotland.

CONTENTS

WHY IT MATTERS

In 2004 I was asked to be one of seven judges for a prestigious poetry promotion organised by the Poetry Book Society. Called Next Generation Poets, it was supposed to identify the twenty "best" new poets published in the UK since 1994. I agreed to be a judge but to my dismay noticed that no black or Asian poets were among the many names submitted. I recommended five whose work had been unfairly overlooked. In the end only one poet made the list, Patience Agbabi.

I raised the issue with Ruth Borthwick, then Director of Literature at the South Bank Centre. She supported an approach I made to Arts Council England. I emailed its Literature Department and suggested they investigate the situation, especially as they fund a lot of poetry presses. Their response was immediate, concerned, positive and gratifying. Ruth and I had a meeting with them and they decided to commission a report as a first step to rectifying this unacceptable state of affairs. Spread the Word Writer Development Agency was commissioned to look into why so few black and Asian poets were being published in this country.

(The terms 'black poet' or 'Asian poet' are, of course, problematic and controversial. Few writers want to be labelled, pigeon-holed, or solely-defined by race or skin colour. But the terms do serve as a convenient shorthand for easy identification.)

The final report, *Free Verse* (2005), was written and researched by Danuta Kean and Melanie Larsen. It revealed that less than 1% of poetry books published in Britain are by black and Asian poets.

This was a shock, even to someone like myself who had long

realised how dire the situation was. How, in the 21st century, in a country such as Britain which has an integrated, racially diverse population, could this tacit colour/culture bar still operate in the poetry publishing world?

I thought back to the 1980s when, in a climate of pioneering arts activism, several poets with a Caribbean heritage were published in Britain, for example, John Agard, Jean 'Binta' Breeze, James Berry, Valerie Bloom, David Dabydeen, Fred D'Aguiar, Linton Kwesi Johnson, Grace Nichols, E.A. Markham (sadly now deceased) and Benjamin Zephaniah. Their publishers were often small, independent presses initially and all are still in print today, along with others who came up in the early 1990s such as Moniza Alvi, Sujata Bhatt, Jackie Kay, Mimi Khalvati and Lemn Sissay. Quite a few, such as John Agard, Imtiaz Dharker, Grace Nichols and Moniza Alvi, are taught on school syllabuses, and all of the above are significant literary figures whose multiple voices and myriad styles have added colour and verve to Britain's poetry scene. More recently poets such as Choman Hardi (Bloodaxe Books), Vahni Capildeo, Anthony Joseph, D.S. Marriott and John Siddique (Salt Publishing and others), Kei Miller (Carcanet), Roger Robinson (flipped eye), Dorothea Smartt and Raman Mundair (Peepal Tree Press) have produced one or two full-length collections. While this may seem like a reasonably hefty list, they still constitute less than 1% of poets published in the UK, and a single imprint, Bloodaxe Books, publishes nearly all the poets not with specialist black and Asian imprints, while several other prominent UK poetry publishers do not publish any black or Asian poets from Britain.

The *Free Verse* report revealed that, when questioned about their selection criteria for publishing new poets, editors unanimously declared that it was based on quality, irrespective of race and gender. Ah, yes, 'Quality' – as if it exists outside the context of history, culture, literary traditions and values, all ingredients that constitute personal taste. As new black and Asian poets are finding access to publishing all but impenetrable, the message is received loud and clear: they are not good enough. In the past they said that about black people who wanted to be footballers, actors, golfers, judges, military officers, pilots and yes, American presidents.

The Free Verse report states: 'If publishers are, as they claim, choosing according to quality and not ethnicity, the law of averages implies a proportion of BME (Black and Minority Ethnic) poets should be picked for publication. But publisher after publisher, both large and small, admits their list is overwhelmingly white.'

It continues: 'The majority of publishers answering the survey desire more representative lists and believe there are BME poets worthy of publication, but somehow that is not happening. Good intentions have gone awry and poets' ambitions and publishers' desires are not producing results. Clearly something is wrong. Explicit racism is not to blame. No poet reported aggressively racist treatment. But many experienced something more subtle. It manifests itself when poets are asked to represent 'The Black Voice' at events, as if one experience represents all Black people, or, as happened to Mimi Khalvati, when rejection slips stated the publisher 'already has one poet to represent the Asian voice'. Khalvati recalls: 'It was ridiculous, especially as the other person's work was so unlike my own.'

The report asks, 'Could the ogre of institutionalised racism be at work in poetry publishing? Could the frustration voiced by the majority of poets spoken to for this survey be the result of cultural barriers – as invisible to publishers as they are frustrating to poets – that limit access to networks, mentors and role models in education and the critical establishment?'

It is natural for editors to want to guard their independence. Yet if the status quo goes unchallenged, nothing changes. That said, the desire for change has to happen from within if it is to have a lasting effect. Tokenism is always transparent. What if poetry publishers, nearly all of whom are white and male, used their position of power and privilege to be more proactive in actively seeking out new voices away from the usual networks? It might mean publishing beyond personal taste. It might mean nurturing talent when it's found, rather than dismissing it as not good enough – yet. It might mean being open to poetry that comes out of unfamiliar cultures and traditions. It might mean being aware that including more diverse voices on a poetry list can only enrich and strengthen it. Faber's publication of Daljit Nagra's first book *Look We Have Coming to Dover!* is a case in point. He is only the second non-white poet to be published in Faber's 80-year history and one hopes that it won't be another 80 years before another such poet makes the list.

What if the editors consider the idea of representation, not as an imposition to be resisted and rejected, but as a demonstration of inclusivity? Editors are the ones with the power to make a difference. The ball is in their court.

Free Verse was published in 2005, full of findings, statistics, conversations and interviews that argued convincingly for change. As is often the way with such reports, the shift it recommended has not yet materialised. Bloodaxe, of course, continues to lead the field. flipped eye publishing, a fiction and poetry press founded by Ghanaian poet and novelist Nii Parkes, continues to publish chapbooks, mainly, by poets of colour. Peepal Tree Press continues to publish international poetry, predominantly from Asia and the Caribbean and has a project called Inscribe to develop black and Asian poets in Yorkshire.

Soon after the report was published I met up with Emma Hewett, Director of Spread the Word. We discussed the idea of a mentoring programme for black and Asian poets who might eventually be taken on by the big publishing houses. An advisory committee was formed: Ruth Borthwick, now director of the Arvon Foundation; Matthew Hollis, poet and editor at Faber; Fiona Sampson, poet and editor of *Poetry Review*; Patience Agbabi, poet; Daljit Nagra, poet and co-editor of this anthology; Emma and myself.

The outcome of our meetings was a two-year national mentoring project for poets called The Complete Works managed by Nathalie Teitler. The ten poets were chosen via process of open application and selection by the committee, who based their decisions on anonymous submissions. The poets are Rowyda Amin, Mir Mahfuz Ali, Malika Booker, Nick Makoha, Karen McCarthy Woolf, Janet Kofi-Tsekpo, Roger Robinson, Denise Saul, Seni Seneviratne and Shazea Quraishi. They were chosen for the quality of their writing and it was also clear that each had their own distinctive poetic voice, quite varied and different to each other.

This anthology showcases their promise and talent. Indeed, what is striking about the poets is their diversity of style and preoccupations. Although they all have backgrounds rooted in both Britain and elsewhere, their poetry cannot be reduced to being representative of a homogenous 'black voice' or 'Asian voice'. Through their poetry the case is made for the multiplicity of voices out there.

At the start of the project each poet chose an individual mentor, an established poet, who would work closely with them in developing their poetry. They are Paul Farley, W.N. Herbert, Mimi Khalvati, Stephen Knight, Pascale Petit, Michael Schmidt, Catherine Smith, John Stammers, Michael Symmons Roberts and George Szirtes. Each mentor has written a commentary introducing the poet's work on these pages. These fascinating commentaries contextualise and explore the poetics of each individual writer and reveal their unique qualities and strengths.

The mentees were also offered a number of poetry seminars such as on 'Lineation' with Mimi Khalvati, on 'Reading as a Writer' with Ruth Padel and John Stammers, and further talks from Alan Jenkins and David Harsent. And they have also undertaken two week-long residential courses at the Arvon Foundation in Yorkshire with Sean O'Brien and Jo Shapcott, and Mimi Khalvati and Pascale Petit.

Although Daljit and I are editors, the poems included here are sometimes the result of editorial decisions shared and negotiated with the mentors.

The development and mentoring process is currently at the halfway stage, yet several of the poets have already had significant achievements: Roger Robinson's second collection, *Suckle* (flipped eye) won the People's Book Prize, Rowyda Amin's pamphlet will be published by Tall-Lighthouse and many of the others have been offered national and international residencies.

We hope that in the next few years the others will complete full-length collections, too and that when they come knocking, the gatekeepers will at last open their doors.

■ **BERNARDINE EVARISTO**

KAREN McCARTHY WOOLF

■ **KAREN McCARTHY WOOLF** was born in London to English and Jamaican parents. Her pamphlet *The Worshipful Company of Pomegranate Slicers* was a Poetry Book Society Pamphlet Choice and was selected as a 2006 Book of the Year in the *New Statesman*, which said her work 'fizzes with intelligence, energy and linguistic invention'.

Karen has presented her work as a writer, editor and critic at a variety of venues including the Barbican, the Purcell Room, South Bank Centre, the Bath Literature Festival and on BBC Radios 3 and 4. Her poetry has been commissioned as an installation for the London Word Festival, exhibited on the London Underground and is anthologised in *New Writing 15* (Granta/British Council, 2007) and *I Am 20 People* (Enitharmon Press, 2007).

In 2005 her period drama *Dido: Queen of Kenwood*, based on the life of a mixed-race girl who grew up in 18th-century London was broadcast on BBC Radio 4. That year she was also writer in residence at the writer development agency Spread the Word and at the Museum of Garden History.

Karen is the editor of two literary anthologies, *Bittersweet: Black Women's Contemporary Poetry* (The Women's Press, 1997) and *Kin* (Serpent's Tail, 2004). She is also a contributing editor and reviewer at the international literary magazine *Wasafiri*, a UK Poetry Editor for the Singapore-based online magazine *Writers Connect*, and recently joined the editorial board at *Magma*. She has taught creative writing for a variety of agencies including the Photographers' Gallery and Arvon. ■

■ MICHAEL SYMMONS ROBERTS:

When I came across Karen McCarthy Woolf's work in her first pamphlet publication, *The Worshipful Company of Pomegranate Slicers*, I was struck by her ambition, wit and sureness of touch. I was impressed by the range of voices interwoven in her poems, at times almost like radio dramas in miniature, and by her evident interest in form. These are rare qualities in first collections.

Karen's more recent poems are rooted in the same territory: the struggle for authentic relationships (with family, friends, colleagues) in a complex urban environment, but she pushes those questions of relationship and responsibility into wider areas of politics, ecology and history. Her continuing exploration of poetic form has given her work a new tightness and energy, and her desire to tell stories in poems has drawn her into longer sequences. Her ability to shift ground, to turn a poem on a shocking and powerful central image – as in 'My Limbs Beat Against the Glass' – demonstrates a growing and justified confidence in her own skill.

Karen's dedication of the poems in this book to 'Otto McCarthy Woolf, born and died 7 August 2009' gives the reader some insight into the shape of Karen's life in the last year. Her poetry was already concerned with love, how close any of us can get to each other, and the risk and fear of the loss of that love. For Karen, after much reflection, it seemed inevitable and fitting to write about Otto's death. This is not a "subject", but an overwhelming event in the poet's life, and the poetic sequence published here is part of her remarkable response to that. ■

Blue Murder: *To yell at the top of one's voice, especially from terror. The expression seems to pun on the French exclamation – 'mor bleu' which is actually a form of 'mort Dieu', 'God's death'.*
BREWER'S DICTIONARY OF PHRASE & FABLE

For Otto McCarthy Woolf, born and died 7 August 2009.

Yellow Logic

1 *The Weather in the Womb*

Upstairs in a room facing north
a summer
         marries immediately.
Our job was to get her to drink.
It took a seismic shift to get changed
         after dinner.

Autumn is head down in the sink.
The trees taste iron and wren
         droppings.
Oh my rustic plectrum!
Your music is
         where the leaf falls.
                  Where it
                  falls

the river hums like a PC.

      Take note
of the ice on the water trough in the yard
and the Eskimo oil from deep sea fish
      caught by a bear
whose coat is a lichen of silver tipped hair
fuzzy as alkanet.

There is a God
      and he dwells in the perfect
horse dung on the bridle path.

Evening is the hardest skin we carry.

II *My Limbs Beat Against the Glass*

I am trapped in a room where my baby dies
and when I try to fight my way out

a Victorian lepidopterist with walrus whiskers
skewers my solar plexus

and pins me to a felt-backed board
so my limbs beat against the glass

like a moth battering a paper lantern
as he tightens the frame to a vacuum.

III *Mor Bleu*

— rushes and there's no more

a whirl of empty dresses —
         in this mudcracked room
                palm frond feathers
          helicopter

          downwards
shallow roots torn
         a broken bird
            song explodes
         on a frequency of earth and lime
                too high to hear

— we haven't got —
         a heart   beat

— haven't got five minutes
a groan of sea
        shushes up on shore

— rushes and there's no —
no *ha ha ha* of music
            and radio
       the thud of workmen
          clatter of hollow poles — scaffolding
a truck in first gear
        footsteps
           school

an O of bells clang-
                    clangs across the river

          and then the hush
                         of marble
               eyes

unseen

               eyes
          unopened

               endlessly

eyes

IV *Mort Dieu*

Our son
dear God
is dead
and gone.
His tomb
was red
with blood
and warm
as tears.
He was
born still.
Was this
dear God
your will?

V *White Butterflies*

Three white butterflies
flutter then land
on the artichoke spikes
in the walled garden.

White sky against the ash.
The wind in the leaves
a rush of sighs.

White lavender
at the edge of the pool.
White hydrangeas
wilted in the bouquet.
White lilies sticky with scent.
White tissues in the box.
White linen on the bed.
White curtains shrunk in the wash.
White muslin squares,
Your tiny white vests, unworn.

VI *Yellow Logic*

Was it because I should have
bought those handmade, pony-hair boots
that swung round my ankles like a mane?
I can't forget Spaghetti Beach
and the gypsy girl with a nose ring
who sold me a rotting shoulder bag
then cursed me.
      Perhaps, my darling boy, we'll meet
at the *piscina municipal* in Murcia,
the one cut into the cliff,
surrounded by thick-bladed grass
green as astro-turf. I'll be lithe and sleek
as I back-flip into the water and pretend
I'm not afraid you'll disappear
like the sun on a so-so afternoon.

ROWYDA AMIN

■ **ROWYDA AMIN** was born in Newfoundland, Canada to parents of Saudi Arabian and Irish origin and has since lived in Riyadh and various parts of England before settling in London, where she is currently a PhD candidate at Birkbeck College, University of London. Rowyda won the *Wasafiri* New Writing Prize for poetry in 2009 and has had poems published in magazines including *Magma*, *Rising* and *Notes from the Underground*. ■

■ CATHERINE SMITH:

Rowyda Amin's lucent, luscious and intriguing poetry is wide-ranging in its scope, with several main themes. It is concerned with exploring the personal and autobiographical; with family, memory, sexuality; with narrative and historical material and intertextuality; with folk and fairy tales, mythology and with science. Although she is also adept at using traditional forms, in this selection the poems are in free verse – always with concise, cadenced rhythm, and a sure-footed appreciation of how the poem's structure can support and enhance its theme.

'Insect Studies' (the title and inspiration for which came from a section of Lafcadio Hearn's *Kwaidan*), is a narrative poem in four stanzas, narrated by a tattoo artist. Lush, sensuous imagery is used to explore the relationship between client and practitioner; the final "scene" enters the realm of the magical, as the client's "butterflies" enter the narrator's skin. This is both an implicitly sexual and magical realist poem, both areas where her talents are obvious. Similarly, in 'Mojave', magical realism, and a fresh take on the creation myth, serves this mythical poem well.

In 'Monkey Daughter', the narrator explores the complexities of family dynamics; the tensions and insecurities in the relationship between a mother and the 'true' daughter, upon the arrival of the "interloper" – the 'baby capuchin', bizarrely named Laura. The monkey – which can symbolise virtuous or foolish aspects of human behaviour – becomes the focus of the mother's love and the "true" daughter's fears.

Family dynamics and memory, recurrent themes, are also visited in the visceral, sensuous 'Grandparents', where the poet explores her wish to excavate/recover elusive memories of the dead – who now exist in sensory images and associations – such as money spiders and 'the turmeric twist of smoke / from my grandfather's shed'. The sparse punctuation gives the poem a breathless, forward-driving energy, with the magical, folk-tale image at the end, 'the chattering / of all the daffodil teeth.'

'Desert Sunflowers' is written in couplets, and demonstrates her interest in history, science and cultural memory – an imagining of how those present at the Trinity atomic bomb tests, 1945, might have acted. The straightforward 'When it was over they blinked at their blind spots' can be contrasted with the sensuous, lyrical final couplet – 'dense fields of black-hearted sunbursts / blossoming between the mountains'.

'Frost Fair', written in longer, more relaxed lines, is also concerned with history, and with the way time can slide over itself; in imagining the Thames frozen over – now, as in a past century. Here, the poet's interest in family and relationships are explored in the wickedly cheerful, 'Crowds scoff hotdogs and candyfloss / cheer as Punch batters Judy with the baby'. The surreal, poignant image evoked by 'Falling snow feathers the whipped bear moonwalking in chains' is typical of this poem's emotional and thematic range. The poem also uses quotations from 'Greensleeves', demonstrating a real flair for intertextuality; finally, we're left with *'And yet thou wouldst not love.'* ■

Mojave

They saw themselves walking toward themselves
over peacock-feather lakes that weren't there,
but they or their reflections disappeared
within touching distance. Father got drunk
using up the booze from the cabin to piss
pleas for help in the sand, but no planes swooped
before it dried. The sand serrated Mother's
eyelids so that she wept rose-tinted tears
that dripped into the daughter's open mouth.
In the morning, they found the girl floating
upside down in the air.
                                They prised open
her mouth and she vomited weeds and fish
that became lizards and hid in the sand.
They buried her and piled up stones
to keep her from floating away. Under the ground,
she listened to the scaly whisperings
of the lizards. Her tongue attuned to the salt
of distant lakes. She grew large, sub-divided,
hatched herself and scattered across the surface
in twelve directions while Mother and Father
crawled on their elbows through the sand,
following themselves in a circle, their bodies
fusing mouth to anus in a writhing ring
as the snake of their mirages swallowed its tail.

Desert Sunflowers

While they waited for the weather to turn, Fermi
offered wagers on the odds of igniting

the atmosphere and destroying the earth
or just New Mexico. Teller made them nervous,

slapping on the sunscreen. Oppenheimer
wore dark glasses like the rest

and held onto a post with damp hands.
He had ten dollars on them failing.

In the control centre, Allison counted down
5-4-3-2-1 NOW! They shielded their eyes

against the flash then saw the mountains lit up
clear as noon by the orange-yellow fireball

that mushroomed blood-red to pink
at ten thousand feet before it dimmed.

When it was over they blinked at their blind spots.
Isidor Rabi passed the whiskey. Bainbridge said

Now we are all sons of bitches. Oppenheimer smiled,
strutted into base camp in his wide-brimmed hat.

By night, rain was falling with the dust
and next morning they saw, all around

the green glass crater, in every section
of the Jornada del Muerto,

dense fields of black-hearted sunbursts,
blossoming between the mountains.

Insect Studies

She flinched only as I began
the black frame of the Emerald Swallowtail
poised to land on a blossom of the cherry branch
that bloomed across her back.

When I'd wiped off the rust of blood
and excess colour and padded her latest with gauze,
she slipped her shirt back on
and we drank coffee
while a teenage boy searched through flash sheets
to find the right kanji for his arm.

She showed me pictures of fritillaries
she wanted inked in the spaces
on her lower back and thighs.
The boy settled on 'death'
and took her place.

See you after payday she said,
but never did except for the night in June
when I woke silver with honeydew
and she stood in the doorway,
her body a flutter of bright little wings
and antennae curling away from her
like cursive script
and the butterflies flew to me,
flattening themselves against my skin,
each eager proboscis
burying deep in the tissues.

Frost Fair

Slideshow faces flicker from the station.
You're following the mood to London Bridge
where taxis cruise black as death's pyjamas.
The Thames you find is glacier silk, shantied
with booths and carousels. Five screaming hens
speed by in a white horse sleigh. Ballad singers
busk their vagrant lines. *Alas my love, you do me wrong.*
Crowds scoff hotdogs and candyfloss,
cheer as Punch batters Judy with the baby.
Hog roasts spit fat on the ice, children watching
with faces pink and hot. *Thy girdle of gold so red.*
Falling snow feathers the whipped bear moonwalking in chains.
It looks at you with marshmallow eyes
and you want to take its arms and zip over the ice,
feel fur on your cheeks, skating against the wind to the estuary
where the ice breaks apart, but you smile, hands in pockets,
and turn to the skittles and acrobats, sugared crepes and hot
        wine.
And yet thou wouldst not love.

Monkey Daughter

On my birthday, my mother takes delivery
of a baby capuchin. All week
she has been converting her study
into a nursery, with a cot
and yellow curtains, cupcake patterned.

She feeds the monkey
warm milk from a bottle,
little chunks of papaya and apple.
Hushes and lulls, names it Laura.
The monkey's scared brown eyes roll like olives.
I want to shake them out of the jar.

Laura wears tiny dungarees
and pinafores, my baby clothes
from the attic, where my parents
had been saving them for grandchildren.
Her photo replaces mine on the fridge.

This one, my mother says, pinning
the monkey's nappy, *will not grow up.*

Grandparents

I need to smell their saffron
so I drag them
out of the earth like soggy bags

hold them to me
mulchy and stained

rotten leaves steeped past yellow
in the dirt

their skulls like a smoker's
once-white ceiling.

I want to dredge their graves
for the crockery broken
in back gardens

split the soil's richness to open
the ruby caches of money spiders and find

the turmeric twist of smoke
from my grandfather's shed that I know

is down there if I dig on
past the chattering
of all the daffodil teeth.

MIR MAHFUZ ALI

■ **MIR MAHFUZ ALI** was born in Dhaka, Bangladesh in 1958. He studied at Essex University. He dances, acts and has worked as a male model and a tandoori chef. As a performer, he is renowned for his extraordinary voice – a rich, throaty whisper brought about by a Bangladeshi policeman trying to silence the singing of anthems during a public anti-war demonstration.

He has given readings and performances at the Royal Opera House, Covent Garden, and other theatres in Britain and beyond. His poetry has appeared in *London Magazine*, *Poetry London*, *Ambit*, *PN Review* and other reputable magazines in the UK. His writing influences are Rabindranath Tagore (1861-1941) and Jibanananda Das (1899-1954). His ancestors were court poets in Delhi – wrote both in Farsi and Urdu. They did not stop writing ghazals even when British artillery shells fell on the Fort during the long siege at the time of the Indian Mutiny of 1857. Mahfuz was shortlisted for the New Writing Ventures Awards 2007. ■

■ PASCALE PETIT:

Mir Mahfuz Ali grew up during the war of liberation in Bangladesh and came to England in 1973, after being shot in the throat by riot police during an uprising. His grandfather was a poet who wrote in Urdu and Farsi and his father edited the prestigious newspaper *The Bangladesh Times*, so Mahfuz had access to world literatures at an early age, including poets such as Lorca, Neruda and Whitman. His influences are mainly Bengali – Tagore, Nazrul Islam, and the more modernist Jibanananda Das. He aims to revive the Bengali tradition but to write it in English.

He writes passionate poetry of witness about first-hand experience of atrocities. The subject matter of 'My Salma' is shocking, quite different from the usually moderate British poem. This is urgent poetry, which feels as though it had to be written and although the lines are musical, the forms are straightforward free verse, as if this is no time for game play-ing. But what strikes most is the linguistic freshness of the descriptions, the sensuous particulars blended with the force of the suffering. There is the lushness of 'her begooni blouse', the sharper realism of the soldier's 'rifle-blue buttocks' and the simpler lyrical lines such as 'when you are full of yourself and blooming'. The traumatic intermingles with the sensory: 'urging me to spit at a woman / as I might spit a melon seed into the olive dust'.

'Midnight, Dhaka, 25 March 1971' bears witness to a war-torn city by assuming the voice of a camera, yet Mahfuz has said: 'I was there when no cameramen were there, so I was the camera, taking pictures with my poetry.' The conceit is multi-layered, and acts as a distancing lens the reader can bear to look through, each photographic shot fresh as an impression on a child's retina. The images are so searing that they must be cooled, so the camera/youth is hardened and has a lake-black Nikon eye. The human and inanimate are interchangeable, the dead piled up to 'the sky's armpits', so traumatic is the incident to the recording self. The final camera-click on a billboard of Guinness is in ironic contrast to the 'dry and bitter dust' of the street. ■

My Salma

Forgive me Badho, my camellia bush,
when you are full of yourself and blooming,

you may ask why, having spent so many years
comfortably in your breasts I still dream of Salma's

just as I did when I was a hungry boy in shorts,
her perfect fullness amongst chestnut leaves.

The long grass broke as I ran, leaving
its pollen on my bare legs.

When the soldiers came, even the wind
at my heels began to worship Salma's beauty.

*

A soldier kicked me in the ribs. I fell
to the ground wailing.

They brought Salma into the yard,
asked me to watch how they would explode

a bullet into her. But I turned my head away
as they ripped her begooni blouse,

exposing her startled flesh. The young soldier
held my head, twisting it back towards her,

urging me to spit at a woman
as I might spit a melon seed into the olive dust.

*

The soldier decorated with two silver bars
and two half-inch stripes was the first to drop his

ironed khaki trousers and dive on top of Salma.
His back arched as she fought for the last leaf

of her dignity. He laughed as he pumped
his rifle-blue buttocks in the Hemonti sun.

Then covered in Bengal's soft soil, he offered
her to the next soldier in line.

They all had their share of her,
dragged her away out of the yard.

I went in search of Salma,
amongst the firewood in the jungle.

*

Stood in the middle of a boot-bruised field,
working out how the wind might lead me to her.

Then I saw against the deepening sky
a thin mangey bitch, tearing at a body with no head,

breasts cut off in a fine lament,
I knew then who she was, and kicked

the bitch in the ribs, the same way
that I had been booted in the chest.

Midnight, Dhaka, 25 March 1971

I am a hardened camera clicking at midnight.
I have caught it all – the screeching tanks
pounding the city under the massy heat,
searchlights dicing the streets like bayonets.
Kalashnikovs mowing down rickshaw pullers,
vendor sellers, beggars on the pavements.
I click on, despite the dry and bitter dust
scratched on the lake-black water of my Nikon eye,
at a Bedford truck waiting by the roadside,
at two soldiers holding the dead by their hands and legs,
throwing them into the back, hurling
them one upon another until the floor
is loaded to the sky's armpits. The corpses stare
at our star's succulent whiteness
with their arms flung out as if to bridge a nation.
Their bodies shake when the lorry chugs.
I click as the soldiers laugh at the billboard on the bulkhead:
GUINNESS IS GOOD FOR YOU
SIX MILLION DRUNK EVERY DAY.

My First Shock at School

Muktar was his name – his tongue
still white with his mother's milk,
and he sucked his thumb in the classroom.
Monsoon music drowned the light of day.
Our Lakeside School was surrounded by black waters.
Water-hyacinth, rice-grass and lotus covered the lake.
Tiffin time. Playground muddy.
We had nowhere to go at break, but watched
how the rain-mist dusted our eyes – a white darkness.
He led me to the back of our school.
We stood at the water's edge.
He took his fleshy shoot out of his pouch.
It was small as a young gherkin,
a yellow flower still attached to its head.
I laughed. He took my hand, pulled it
and asked me to touch, as if to take the flower
with the ant that hid in its pollen.
I snatched my hand away.
He wanted to slide mine out of my blue shorts,
measure it against his.
I refused. He insisted again,
said it was tiny and soft as a leech.
I reached out into the darkness of my pants.
His eyes sparkled as if he'd just seen a spikenard bloom.

Bidisha on the Wall

Her picture on the west wall
makes it hard to forget
how special Bidisha was.
I feel like breaking every mirror
in the house, as she sits thoughtfully
on the edge of a balloon-back chair.
This woman is not coming down to me
from the cold wall into my warm bed.
It is tough to look at her
without recalling the incident
that pulled her boat towards the heavy mouth
of the long furtive river of the fish-valley.
I have no idea how she let go the hands
of the one she danced with until the ship capsized.
All I know is that she was in that disco boat
catching the morphine moons
in her glasses of champagne,
over the cold-tongued, thousand-eyed Thames.

Still Birth

After so many miscarriages
this bone-shine baby
with its heart pounding
like a moondark dawn,
with a promise of dark hair and teak eyes
and little more than one foot long.
As she lay on the silver tray
I could see where she'd have her dimple
and how it'd pull me into the whorl
that'd catch my breath.
For a moment I forgot
she had no river-buds in her pulse
and no zit of lights in her eyes.
Yet it seemed she laughed.
I picked up my girl gently,
her marble head tipped back
in the cup of my hot hand.
Her arms didn't spread
into the wings of a seagull.
I let her float in the room's sky
as I shook her in my hands.
Then I wrapped up her tiny body
in swaddling cloth
and put her in a Jones shoe box.

DENISE SAUL

■ **DENISE SAUL** was born in London. A poet, fiction writer and visual artist of Guyanese and Ethiopian ancestry, she was awarded the George Viner Trust award for journalism. Her *White Narcissi* (flipped eye publishing) was the Poetry Book Society Pamphlet Choice for Autumn 2007. Her poetry has been published in a variety of US and UK magazines and anthologies. Denise views poetry as an exploration of the self. 'It is through this process that the poet experiences a complete oneness with the universe. It is also a journey of the hero/ine which involves initiation, transformation and formation.' ■

■ JOHN STAMMERS:

Denise Saul's unusual and varied work exhibits a range of wide sweeps. She can bring within her scope anything from the smallest flash of luminescence to great caves and valleys. Her vision also has the capacity to span the world as it moves across from Paris to the Afar Valley, to the heart of Africa and beyond. Time itself can also come within the ambit of what she chooses to notice. Her poems will on many occasions shift back and forth between the present and the near-past. From there she can even be seen to make the mighty leaps: with her vision deep enough to take in the palaeontological.

In a more detailed sense her poems also consider all sorts of variety of object. In this regard, many of her poems – for very good examples see such poems as 'Quartz Cave' or 'Moon Jelly' – display a kind of balanced brittle beauty. These are portrayed with a careful poise that precisely fits with their subject matter, mimicking the delight in substances from which such things are made.

Denise Saul's formal approach is by and large a sparely written free verse. Once more this clean, crafted writing complements her way of dealing with her subject matter. It is as if holding a precious object in her hand and turning it over and over in her regard. She does this in such a way as to reveal to us her own perception. In this way her poems often feel much like a precious object themselves. ■

City of Coffee and Rain

Thirty years on, I find you on the birch tree.
You must have soared to the top
in a cloak of copper feathers.
Your man-face caught in the north wind.
I have heard that call before in St Germain.
One hoot outside the house takes me
back to the night you vanished.
It is said that the Guyanese spirit walks backwards.
When the sky goes dark, rain falls.

Some things have a double life,
a twin entity which rises from light.
Father, you live in a parallel universe.
To bring you back into this world, I throw
harare beans into a small pot
and walk three times around the kitchen.

The room smells of roasted beans.
At the climax of the twelfth hour, my father,
a white-clad figure appears at the table.
I look ahead to watch him walk
backwards down the hallway.
Through the front door, he departs.

Brown froth flows from a porcelain cup.
This is a city of coffee and rain.
I take any drops of water that fall.

The sound of the river Seine trickles into my ear.
I walk in these copper-plated shoes
to Pigalle, yet water speaks for you, father.
I hear the river as the sound of satin static.
At Rive Gauche, water swells and flows slowly
down to my feet through a tunnel of bricks.

Quartz Cave

As if the day still depends on it for brightness,
the sky above begins to lighten.
Veins of iron ore crack open granite,
stalactites burst downward into white light.
Deeper into the silence, a smell of salt
covers crystal rafters, and then
rises from this geode, rises
from orange earth through a fault.
The basalted surface warms overground.
Night will lie down in this country
as water falls from the candlestick.

Moon Jelly

Its luminescence belongs here in the sea.
Throwback from coral, this
polyp floats on the surface:
an outcast, seven inches
of nerves, no brain or heart.
Four arms hang down from a bell.
A drifter – agile, scyphozoan –
a blob of streaks and patterns,
its light in the last hour.

One

Step back now and look again at the femur.
Turn the bone upright and it is a glyph,
a perfect representation of the number one.
The research team names her part-skeleton
Australopithecus afarensis.
More shovels arrive in the morning.

The next day, workers dance to that Beatles'
song, *Lucy in the Sky with Diamonds*,
playing on the tape recorder.
They drink a bottle of Shiraz; they christen her Lucy.
I raise a glass of tej over the Hadar site and sniff
forest honey that grandmother mixed
with gesho leaves to make wine.

This reminds me of grandmother.
Grave-soil and termites fell from her mouth:
don't ask me again about where we come from.
Because her body was covered in skin, hard as flint,
she sometimes called herself Stone-Dress.
I begged her not to leave the village.

Grandmother wore black obsidian,
even though the desert cracked beneath her feet.
The belt was carved from the upper delta
and an emerald stream ran down her back.
When she carried a bag of chicken bones,
she clapped and chanted *sangoma, sangoma, sangoma.*
Grandmother placed the bones on a shrine
but could not read what they said.

Come closer and see several hundred fragments
of ourselves scattered across the Afar region.
They say that the number one is linked
to a noble number, the whole which is made
of many parts: ulna, jaw and teeth.
It is the number of the first mother.

ROGER ROBINSON

■ **ROGER ROBINSON** is a Trinidadian poet and playwright who has lived in London for 20 years. He has performed worldwide and is an experienced workshop leader and lecturer on poetry. He was also chosen by Decibel as one of 50 writers who have influenced the Black-British writing canon over the past 50 years. He has received commissions from the Theatre Royal Stratford East, The National Trust, London Open House and the National Portrait Gallery. He has toured extensively with the British Council including Vietnam, the Philippines, Argentina, Bulgaria, Greece, India, the Czech Republic and Mozambique. His workshops have been nominated for a Gulbenkian Prize and he was part of the Webby Award winning team of online workshops for The Barbican's *Can I Have a Word*.

In 2007 he received a grant from Arts Council England. He has published a book of short fiction, *Adventures in 3D* (2001), and two poetry collections, *Suitcase* (2004) and *Suckle* (2009) under flipped eye's Waterways imprint. Until 2000, Roger Robinson was programme co-coordinator of Apples and Snakes poetry agency. *Suckle* won the People's Book Prize in 2009.

Website: www.rogerrobinsonbooks.com ■

■ PAUL FARLEY:

Roger Robinson's poetry is preoccupied with memory, perception and revelation. He is a skilled fuser of narrative momentum with lyrical description, creating poems that can beguile and arrest while never losing sight of what James Wright referred to as the 'pure clear word': his work manages to be both convincingly rich and textured yet is blessed by a clarity and focus that makes it approachable and imaginatively inhabitable. He often returns to aspects of a Trinidadian upbringing, or more specifically, its elements of community and belonging, perhaps most obviously apparent in this selection's poems that are set in school, but also easily detectable in a poem like 'The Stand Pipe', a very physical locus, or 'Mr Lee Wah Moves Mountains', where the local topography itself is under threat and in disintegration.

'The Stand Pipe' uses the local source of fresh water as a refracting lens, pulling together images from childhood that are convincingly rendered: the iron buckets, the gossip in the queue, the chlorine smell of bleach, all place the reader in the sensual middle of things, as the stand pipe itself comes to simply but brilliantly emblemise the rhythms of the day. But things are deceptively simple: look how the poem's speaker, in 'starched white shirt and pleated pants', already seems distanced, separate somehow from the flow of things, a distance that subtly offsets the general breaking down of public and private space, where men strip down to their underpants 'and lather up right there', eventually pulling the speaker (and the reader) up short in the final line's returned gaze. In 'Griffiths', the poem's speaker is again watching, though this time the scene is much more kinetic and urgent,

Griffiths's dad's minatory march up the college hill setting the tone for something far more unsettling and darkly revelatory.

The past in these poems is often made alive to us, unfinished, and their limpidity is all the more impressive when we consider that this is a writer interested in how we look at, recall and participate in our pasts, what we misremember, and how difficult or complicated at times it might also be to return to them. He often admits broader currents to flow through his Caribbean, such as the mercantile rapaciousness that brought, and brings, both traders in sugar and sex tourists ('The New La Diablesse'). In recent years, he has grown increasingly interested in the formal region that exists – to put it crudely – between page and stage; a brilliant performer of his own poems, he is exploring the measures and figures of speech and formal written language that issue from a common source: the body. ■

The Stand Pipe

Right there, on the corner, was where
you'd fill your iron bucket if you had no water.

Every morning on my way to school
I'd see people waiting for their chance.

In my starched white shirt and pleated
pants I waited for a taxi, looking at them.

Their lives seemed so simple. Days started
with getting two buckets of clean water.

Wives would gossip until it was their turn.
Kids would walk uphill in measured steps

with a filled bucket half their size.
Sometimes grown men would strip off,

down to their underpants, and lather up
right there – blue soap and frothy beards.

Naked tots were baptised in public,
mothers shampooing shapes in their hair.

Gallons of water flowed as women washed
their families' clothes, their fists riding

the ridges of the scrubbing board, making clothes
white again with the chlorine smell of bleach.

Now a mother is walking away with a full bucket
for her coffee, a naked baby perched on her hip.

And a man with grey hair pulls white pockets
out of his khakis and sees me looking at him.

Griffiths

Griffiths's dad marched up the college hill.
A man with an angry walk, a man with a stick.
He grabbed Griffiths – the school thug – by his shirt,
pulling him to the centre of the football field,
their dark brown skins clear against the sandy field.

His father raised his switch and we heard
the swoosh and the thwack of each stroke.
It looked like a man beating a small replica
of himself. The backswing of each lash so high
it seemed to be pointing at the relentless sky.

Griffiths stood upright with his hands
on his head. Soon the teachers stopped teaching
and student heads crowded the windows.
He was a hated boy in the halls of school.
He robbed the younger and weaker of money.

But nobody wanted this. After the fifteenth stroke
some boys and teachers were in tears, still watching
this very public execution. By the twentieth stroke
we noticed our principal's paunch bobbing
quickly towards the scene and physically stopping

the beating. The father threw down the cane,
turned and started walking without looking back.
Griffiths collapsed into the principal's hug.
O forgive the bleaching sun, O forgive the father.
O forgive the witnesses, O Griffiths, Griffiths.

Mr Lee Wah Moves Mountains

San Fernando Hill was being slowly scraped
away to gravel by yellow bulldozer claws.

Vice Principal, Lee Wah, planned a protest;
all people had to do was grab a placard.

Mr Lee Wah wrote the Bristol board signs: *Don't
Kill Our Hill* – stapled to broomsticks.

On the day, there was only him and the signs.
He waited and waited and nobody else came.

Finally in the centre of La Romain roundabout
he grabbed all ten placards and stood in the hot sun.

A one-man protest as cars zoomed past and beeped.
People pointed and laughed. The newspapers came.

The headlines on the next day told of a madman's
protest. Jokes were made about him at lunch breaks.

There were calls to stop him from teaching.
That school year he barely left his office;

he just sat at his desk, with a thousand-yard stare,
his spirit ground down to rock and rubble.

Miss Jagroop

The heavy curve of your breasts grazed our shoulders
as you checked over our comprehension homework.
You'd pull some pouting pose every five minutes
with your butter fat rear spreading all over our desks.
Did you smell our musky adolescent scent?
Did you breathe us all in? All our stale breaths?
We liked you as much as we were embarrassed.
The charged atmosphere made us drunk with desire.
But when you ran your hands through Gerard's hair
and told him that he was becoming so handsome,
that all the young ladies must be queuing up for him.
When you held his gaze and bit your bottom lip
for three or four silent seconds, the only thing we could do
was look at our muddy shoes.

The New La Diablesse

(for the sex tourists of Tobago)

I wear my long white cotton skirt
so no man will see my cow foot.

I can smell the death on each man who looks
at me with that lustful eye. It's a scent

much like the smell of mould, semen
and wet earth. That smell is what I live for.

The ones who can control their nature
can see me for what I really am:

The faithful, the very old, the very young,
some of the clergy and the strictly gay,

they can hear the clicking of my hoof,
see the hop and drop nature of my walk.

To those young men seeking sex,
husbands cheating on their wives. The vain,

the opportunists, the experimenters, the kinky –
I am the bait for hell, the ecstatic funk of death.

Perverted doom, freaky eternal suffering heat.
I'm the La Diablesse. Burn, burn with my love.

SHAZEA QURAISHI

■ **SHAZEA QURAISHI** was born in Pakistan, emigrated to Canada aged ten, and lived in Madrid before moving to London. Her poems have been published in anthologies and magazines in the UK and the US. She works as a writer, translator and teacher of creative writing and literacy. ■

■ STEPHEN KNIGHT:

There is an intriguing collision between the archaeological and the lyrical in Shazea Quraishi's series of poems, 'The Courtesan's Reply', inspired by Manomohan Ghosh's translations from the Sanskrit of *The Caturbhani*. Written around 300 BC, the four monologues which make up *The Caturbhani* follow a narrator as he walks through the courtesans' quarter, commenting on the women he meets and engaging them in a one-sided conversation. The props and rituals bestow on these poems an exotic otherness, but the emotions they explore are timeless. 'The Sixty-four Arts' and 'The Days of Chandragupta Maurya' emerge from research into the period, playfully drawing on found material, while 'Tambulasena' is one example of a courtesan's voice liberated, and allowed to speak after centuries of silence. This need to give a voice to the voiceless is present, too, in 'Mwanza, Malawi', an unsentimental poem of an all-too-familiar situation. ■

THE COURTESAN'S REPLY

*Ah, the supreme beauty of the courtezans' quarter which
is the work-shop of love! Houses are as high as the towering
Kailāsa mountains (and) their windows are being pressed
down by the plump breasts of courtezans...*

M. GHOSH, *Glimpses of Sexual Life in Nanda-Maurya India*
(a translation of *The Caturbhani*)

The Sixty-four Arts

And so, a courtesan of pleasant disposition,
beautiful and otherwise attractive,
master of sixty-four arts
including music, dancing, acting, singing,
the composition of poetry,
flower-arrangement and garland-making,
the preparation of perfumes and cosmetics,
dress-making and embroidery, conjuring
and sleight of hand,
logic, cooking, sorcery,
fencing with sword and staff, archery, gymnastics,
carpentry, chemistry, architecture
and minerology,
the composition of riddles, tongue-twisters
and other puzzles, gardening, writing in cipher,
languages, making artificial flowers
and clay modelling,
training fighting cocks, partridges
and rams, and teaching parrots and mynah-birds to talk...
such a courtesan will be honoured by the King, praised
by the learned, and all will seek her favours
and treat her with consideration.

The Days of Chandragupta Maurya

were split into sixteen hours
of ninety minutes each.

In the first,
he arose and prepared himself by meditation;
in the second,
he studied the reports of his agents
and issued secret instructions;
he met with his councillors in the third hour
and in the fourth,
attended to state finances and national defence;
in the fifth,
he heard the petitions and suits of his subjects
and in the sixth hour, bathed
and dined and read religious literature.
He received taxes and tribute
and made official appointments in the seventh hour.
In the eighth,
he met his council again
and heard the reports of his spies and courtesans.
The ninth hour was devoted to relaxation
and prayer,
while the tenth and eleventh hours were given to military matters
and the twelfth to secret reports.
In the thirteenth hour,
the king indulged in an evening bath and a meal,
and for the next three hours he slept
– but never in the same bed twice.

Tambulasena

In the beginning
my whole body was covered with skin
hard as rock. Then he came

and his mouth
running over me was a river, cool and quick
with small silver fish.

Night after night
he shaped me
and smoothed me

down
to velvet
bones.

    *

Now I bathe while he watches,
his eyes
fireflies on my skin.

I bend over,
my hair a curtain of water
between us.

I let him towel me dry,
his strokes soft at first, then brisk
like a cloth shining a lamp.

Water drips down
my back. He grasps the rope
of my hair and climbs.

Mwanza, Malawi

I am Edith. I am eight.
I have two brothers, Jomo
and David. When we are hungry
my mother holds us
with her body and her eyes.
Some nights I dream the same dream
– my mother covered in flies.

I jump out of the dream
leaving my mother alone
in the dark and the heat.
This happens again and again
until the dream-me holds her eyes open,
puts one foot in front of the other
– goes like this to my mother
because of how much she hates flies –

and reaching her sees
a fine, black shawl covers her
with shiny, black beads
running over her like rain…
      and my mother is sleeping
      in the cool of its shade.

MALIKA BOOKER

■ **MALIKA BOOKER** is a British writer of Guyanese and Grenadian parentage, who writes poetry, plays and solo monologues. Her poems are widely published in anthologies and journals including *Bittersweet: Contemporary Black Women's Poetry* (The Women's Press, 1998), *Wasafiri* (2000), *The Penguin Anthology of New Black Writing* (2000), *India International Journal* (2005), and *Atlas: New Writing* (Crossword Press, 2006). She has been a writer in residence for Hampton Court Palace, Croydon Museum and the Center for Slovenian Literature as well as an Arts Council Fellow at the India International Centre in Delhi.

Malika is the founder of Malika's Kitchen, a writers' collective based in London which offers weekly writers' surgeries, and publishing opportunities in anthologies. The influential Kitchen was established in August 2000 and is successfully supporting multicultural writers in their development of craft. She has run creative writing courses for organisations including Pembroke College, the Arvon Foundation, and is now a creative writing tutor at City Lit. Her collection *Breadfruit* was published by flipped eye in 2007, and was a Poetry Book Society Pamphlet Choice. She is currently working on her first full-length collection. ■

■ W.N. HERBERT:

Malika Booker's poetry is grounded in two sound structural principles, and driven by two engaging thematic concerns.

The formal ground of her work is at once narrative and rhapsodic — that is, her writing both compulsively tells stories, and, equally intensely, sings to us. Both the tales and the manner of their telling are arresting and memorable, from the horrified focus on violent detail in 'Pepper Sauce' to the effortless keening note of 'Earth's Salt'.

Her subject-matter is both familial and genealogical, that is, she draws deeply on her own experience and memories in order to make that leap into the historical imagination which marks out any distinctive voice.

This crossroads of scope and technique is a very good place for a poet to be, particularly in a contemporary culture where fixity of any sort, whether of form or identity, can seem a type of nostalgia. Her work, on the contrary, reaches back into her past only in order to reach out to her audience with renewed vigour.

The two tugs on every writer's sleeve – of their own immediate experience and those ghosts of others' rites of passage – are beautifully balanced in her writing. Her particular heritage of Guyana, Grenada, Brixton and New York allows her to move from intimate reminiscence to the opposition of larger symbolic structures. Whip and cutlass, bird and pepper, historic and personal trauma: the scattered seeds of one are seen in the intense growth of the other.

Above all, this is a poetry captivated by the resonance of language: its ability to evoke tangible, intelligible emotion through musicality and subtle shifts in register, and its capacity for enfolding whole psychologies in one phrase, whole cultures in a single image.

The distance between the 'splek and splak' of an onomatopoeic rope and the rasping swear-words of an abusive grandmother (*'Rasshole! Scunt! Whore!'*) is reduced to the flick of a page, while the angry yet somehow redemptive lilies on an overseer's grave seem woven into the tender braiding of a grim old woman's hair.

This is work which doesn't have to raise its voice to compel us, and which achieves most poets' secret desire: by looking without sentiment, and through listening without preconception, it has learnt how to carry a tune. ■

Overseer's Lament

1

The overseer dead and he whip sprout
scarlet lilies. Whole cane fields bowed,
yea he who wield whip with skill dead,
he who hit them roped bodies wearing blindfold,
he who lash don't miss, dead.

He who sing, *this job is too sweet*, as he fleck,
bloody raindrops from blistering skin gone
causing women to raise up they red petticoats
and dance, trampling he gravesite

while mosquitoes refuse to suck blood
and fireflies lose their light.

2

He death suck earth dry: weeds run riot
in burial ground, cat whips sprout scarlet lilies,
machetes pound stone, lips drown rum,
and home made spirit.

He disappeared from their thoughts
in a finger click. That was one piece of no funeral
where Angie wrap that long skirt tight
so she could sway to leaves clapping
on the trees where she used to hang and swing
licks raining on her skin like scattered rice.
Oh the splek and splak of that rope!

Now she prays to Gods to pelt him
with hard rock, to peel he skin
from he bones, make he crawl like swine.
This day when the mosquitoes strike
and the fireflies cease to glow.

3

Wickedness crumble he body to dust in a finger click
Who beat drum and chant themselves into trance.
Who plant flower seed with light heart. Who talk
to Jumbie, begging them to whip he hard down there,
beat he with bamboo, make he body bear red hibiscus,
he face turn ripe tomato, make his seed dry and burn.

Oh now he dead life sweet like ripe cane
and children's laughter fresh like spring water.

Earth's Salt

Singing *I'll fly away home*, them elders took flight,
gone just so. Flocks of runaway slaves flew back
to Africa, dressed in white calico, bright as angels.

They left armed only with starched backs,
guided by starlight, singing all the way home.
Old people used to say, *We are earth's salt, let none*

pass your lips. Put salt on bird tail to ground he,
make he can't fly, make he easy to catch. We kissed
our teeth, ate salt beef and now we can't fly

home in white by the dark of night. We stick to earth
like Lot's wife pillar. Now runaways are dog bait,
hunted and fetched back, now we dream of death

when we spirit will fly to glory as John Crow
pick flesh clean and those left alive sing, *One fine*
morning when my life is over, I will fly away home.

Plait

That house over by Buxton train line. The house with the wooden front steps and old rocking chair. Those steps where you followed Mum, heaping curses like red ant bites, spewing, *Rasshole! Scunt! Whore!* Your son had an outside woman? So what! Mum ran ashamed, necks craned windows as you *peppered* her skin with cuss, till she got into the flagged-down taxi on the highway.

Years later mum tells me the story after I ask her to go back to Guyana with me. The entire plane journey mum mutters *Wicked woman!* We walk up those same wooden chairs, the divorced wife, the scared granddaughter. At ninety-six you could claim fifty years. That day I saw you sit in the rocking chair, then my mother part your hair, pour coconut oil, massage then plait, her fingers caressing strands.

It's water under the bridge, she tells me later, I can't walk past the wounds, can't talk past the men I froze beneath, your words branded under the skin inside my thighs, legs spread out like a whores. Oh Mother, I watch you plait the hair of the old woman I wanted to love me years ago.

Pepper Sauce

I pray for that grandmother, grinding her teeth,
        one hand pushing in fresh, hot peppers, seeds and all, turning
the handle of the old iron mill, squeezing the limes, knowing
        they will burn and cut raw like acid.

She pours in vinegar, gets Anne to chop five onions with a bulb of
                                                                garlic,
        Chop them up real fine, girl, you hear?
and Anne dicing and crying, relieved that no belt has blistered her skin,
        no knife handle smashed down onto her knuckles
until they bleeding for stealing money from she grandmother purse.

        I hear she made Anne pour
in oil and vinegar and stir up that hot sauce, how she hold she down,
                                                                I hear
        she tied that girl to the bedposts, strung her out naked,
like she lying there on a crucifix, I hear
        she spread she out then say,
        I go teach you to go and steal from me today, Miss Lady.

I hear she scoop up that pepper sauce out of an enamel bowl,
        and pack it deep into she granddaughter pussy,
I hear there was one piece of screaming in the house that day,
                                                                Anne bawl

        till she turn hoarse, bawl
        till the hair on she neighbour skin raise up, bawl
        till she start to hiss through her teeth, bawl
        till she mouth make no more sound,
        I hear how she turn raw, how that grandmother leave her
                                                        there all day,
        I hear how she couldn't walk or talk for weeks.

SENI SENEVIRATNE

■ **SENI SENEVIRATNE**, born and raised in Leeds, Yorkshire, is of English and Sri Lankan heritage. She has been writing poetry since her early teens and was first published in 1989. Her poetry and prose is published in the UK, Denmark, Canada and South Africa. Her poem 'Cinnamon Roots' won second prize in the Margot Jane Memorial Poetry Prize, Onlywomen Press. She has given readings, performances and workshops in Cape Town, Vancouver, New York, Washington, Philadelphia, San Francisco, Los Angeles and around England.

Her poetry was broadcast on radio and recorded on audio-tape, *Climbing Mountains*, and CD, *Seven Sisters*. She has recently released a CD of poetry and song. Her photography appeared in *Feminist Arts News*, Autograph Open Photography Show, Signals Changing exhibition and in a solo exhibition, 'Moving Words'.

Her collaborations include: a mixed media installation, 'Memoried Mosaics' which was exhibited in Sheffield's Open Up event in 2004 and at Outwood Grange College, Wakefield; an art song for piano and voice, 'Dandelion Clocks', commissioned for Leeds Lieder Festival and performed in October 2005; 'A Wider View', verse accompanied by saxophone quartet, commissioned for Leeds launch of architecture week, June 2006.

Her debut collection, *Wild Cinnamon and Winter Skin*, published in 2007 by Peepal Tree Press, offers a poetic landscape that echoes themes of migration, family, love and loss and reflects her personal journey as a woman of mixed heritage. She is currently working on her second collection. ■

■ MIMI KHALVATI:

Seni Seneviratne proudly resists any pressure to be pigeon-holed and her complex history, together with the many hats she wears – writer, singer, photographer, psychotherapist – allow her to be open to facing multiple directions. Her first collection demonstrated the ease with which she crosses continents and centuries and in her recent work Seni continues to explore her versatility, both in subject matter and style. But throughout, her synthesising imagination is evident, and her drive towards integrity.

On themes of family history, search for identity, love and loss, race and class, there are personae poems, poems informed by events in the public arena, cross-arts collaborations, dialect and dream poems, song-like lyrics, written both in free verse and fixed forms. Seni is currently working on an ambitious long narrative, 'The Piano Man' (not included here), echoing terza rima and referencing David Constantine's *Caspar Hauser*. This ambitiousness is belied by her use of language: her natural diction and syntax, quiet turns of thought, lyrical cadences and supple changes of tense. Such transparency allows her not simply to empathise with but to speak from the same side of the fence as her subject, from within the same enclosure.

Seni's early love of the war poets, Sassoon and Owen in particular, her years as a political activitist, performances of folk songs, recent work with victims of trauma, prove the solid ground of the political passion that informs her work. 'Sitting for the Mistress', inspired by a painting in the National Gallery in an exhibition to commemorate the bicentenary of the abolition of the slave trade, is written in the voice of the black child servant of the Duchess of Portsmouth. The formality of the painting is reflected in the formal choice of the sequence: five blank verse sonnets, which counterpoint the simplicity of the child's voice. Without being representational, pictorial elements are conveyed through the child's intense focus on sense images in the face of increasing distress. The tableau-like frame of each of the sittings mirrors the numbness, lack of agency, that often result from rupture and trauma, while the inner drama is played out through the metaphor of the blackbird.

Seni's images, subservient to her line of enquiry, often reflect the way that poems themselves come slowly into focus. In 'Montefegatesi' and 'Roquebrun', the sense of space in which the poems hang, gently pivoting, is suggestive of what is left out: the story of the speaker placed within a community where the sense of scale, the small human, the large other-worldly, provides the perspective. Seni is also a love poet, and 'L'inconnue de la Seine', about a young woman's suicide, is radiant with its desire for dissolution, loss of self in the other, for the bliss of anonymity.

These poems emanate from an absolute faith in the power of poetry to create change, in hearts if not in minds, and Seni's celebrations and outrage from a sensibility that keeps contrarieties in balance. ■

Sitting for the Mistress

Portrait of Louise Keroualle, Duchess of Portsmouth, French Mistress of Charles II, posing with her black child servant (detail), Pierre Mignard, 1682

FIRST SITTING

Blackbird lives inside me – the mistress knows.
She calls me her *petite merlette*, tells me
I mustn't worry because inside my black skin
is a soul as white as the pearls she has tied
so tight around my neck. She says I was three
when she washed the devil away and if I do
bad things she'll have to clip my blackbird wings.
The mistress says I must stand beside her while
Monsieur Mignard makes us up with colours,
that we will be a painting in a gilded frame,
hanging in the halls of the Palace of Whitehall,
her skin lead-white against the lamp-black of mine.
My head begins to spin and Monsieur shouts,
Tilt your chin up! Look at the mistress, not me!

SECOND SITTING

There are feathers everywhere. I sweep them
into small piles far down below my ribs
and smile like the mistress tells me. She has
a face like stone that never smiles. Parched lips
stretch out across dry teeth and pull my cheeks.
The face very close in my dream was squeezing mine
as if our cheeks would melt, tears trickling over me
and the mouth kissing. Blackbird starts to tremble
and then the feathers blow: They clog my throat.
When I cough them out the mistress laughing
says I bark like one of the King's spaniels,
Merlette aboie comme un chien! I count

the clouds still drifting in a painted sky
behind her head till Blackbird falls asleep.

THIRD SITTING

Blackbird sleeps while Monsieur Mignard mixes
colours in his pots of clay. My hand's
too small to hold this shell that's full of pearls.
If I shake, the shell tips up and the pearls fall,
the mistress will be angry. One red jewel,
two red jewels, three – drip from her dress.
Blackbird rouses. The mistress rests her arm
across my back, so light a touch, a tickle
on my shoulder. A touch, a lift, strong arm
round my legs, a hand cupped in my armpit,
fingers pressing my back. Blackbird flutters.
Heavy eyes count her back to sleep. One red
jewel, two red – Mistress nips my shoulder.
Look at me and smile, Merlette! You'll spoil the picture!

FOURTH SITTING

Blackbird is learning to be still, she watches
Monsieur Mignard as he watches me. The mistress
has blue sleeves that drape like open curtains,
the swirls on her golden dress are falling leaves.
The coral chafes my fingers, rough as the blanket
we hide under in the damp room that smells
of the big grey water. At night I push my fist
into my mouth, bite my knuckles till I see
Maman. She's an obechi tree. I claw
at her, my leg reaching to find a foothold
but she's being dragged away smaller and smaller
and then she disappears. Blackbird wails,
her wings screaming at the criss-cross window.
She thuds down. I suck in breath, stay very still.

FIFTH SITTING

Blackbird wants to teach me how to fly
over the palace gardens. There are bitter
berries hidden in the swish of leaves
beside the golden sundial that the mistress
calls *les mûres de ronce* – she rolls the words
like pearls on her tongue. She sits on her velvet stool
and tells me I must be *comme une statue*.
Blackbird pecks my inside skin so my legs
begin to shake. She spreads her wings, pushes
at my ribcage, whirls into the sky screeching.
I want to stop my ears but my hands are full,
my cheeks sting, and I can't find Blackbird
until I hear her call *Maman, Maman!*
You've no Maman, I cry, *you're much too wicked.*

Roquebrun

On such an early morning in July,
a woman would have walked
the river path, past the silent frogs
still drowsy in the undergrowth,
would have seen the village houses
up ahead clinging to the cliffs,
then walked faster than the river's flow
towards the smell of baking bread.

What's altered isn't just the dream
that disappeared in the shaft of sunlight
spilling through the shutters where
I watched the flies spin a dizzy dance
but the way I noticed that I noticed
for the first time, hanging figs, spiked coats
on unripe chestnuts and bleeding hearts
crowding the river's edge.

L'inconnue de la Seine

There was a swell on the surface of the Seine that day
making faces at me. So I blew kisses at an open mouth

and whispered, 'Drown me peaceful, drown me slow.'
I wanted the time, you see, to float undead through Paris,

I could have choked on a glass of milk as a child
and missed this opportunity. Don't call it suicide

as if it's a tragedy. This was the first time in my life
I had been in control of anything. Imagine, not dying

but dissolving, becoming a river. Was I afraid?
Not of the fall. I was afraid of the Water Police,

the way they walk along the river, any one of them
could have seen me floating, but nightfall saved me.

Before the river had me, I had one last look at the stars.
'Just look at you,' I said, 'already dead and still shining.'

Montefegatesi

Late September and still hot. The door's creak
echoes as we step into the cool of candle wax
and faded incense. Who built such tiny churches
high in cobbled villages, statues filling every corner?

Death has been up close all year. On the journey
a winding road dropped perilously to one side
and we held our breath, not so much praying
as remembering the beliefs of those we'd lost.

Now, as the sun shines through the colours
of Judgement Day above the marble altar,
Our Lady of Perpetual Succour holds out her arms.
We walk towards her, light candles for our dead.

NICK MAKOHA

■ **NICK MAHOHA** was born in Uganda, and fled the country with his mother during the Idi Amin dictatorship. He has lived in Kenya and Saudi Arabia, and currently resides in London. His writing deals with displacement, loneliness and the im-pact of forced exile. His first pamphlet, *The Lost Collection of an Invisible Man*, launched the imprint mouthmark in 2005 under award-winning publisher flipped eye. He has presented his work at many international events and toured for the British Council in Finland, the Czech Republic, the US and the Netherlands. Nick's poem 'Vista' was commissioned by Tate Remixed as a short film to interpret the Turner Prize 2008. It reflects on how controversy surrounding the Turner Prize is a great thing for stirring artistic debate. The Theatre Royal Stratford commissioned Nick to write a one-man show, *My Father & Other Superheroes*. Fusing lyrical poetry and Homeric theatre, the show explores how a man was raised by pop culture in the absence of his father. ■

■ GEORGE SZIRTES:

Nick and I discussed and redrafted a great many poems during our meetings, including the ones included here. His intelligence was admirable. Sometimes things fell out just right, or nearly right, the first time; but I liked it just as much when things weren't quite right, when the ambition to articulate something just out of reach was still searching, occasionally stumbling, because it saw the valuable, the important, the vital, and knew it worth chasing.

I like energy and dissatisfaction. Best of all is the moment when all that energy and dissatisfaction produce, construct, come upon, a form that holds, explores and embodies some necessary, valuable truth. Nick's best poems do just that: they don't rest easy. They resist pigeon holing. They are vivid, almost gleaming narratives in lyric form, narratives that deal with hard things in politics and relationships and see those terms as mutually contingent.

The very first poem of his I read was 'Prayers for exiled poets'. The epigraphs from Vallejo and Neruda were interesting. They weren't just bragging. The language was certain of itself – faintly biblical, large of scale, but the theme itself was large of scale. It was reach that impressed me – it looked to comprehend a proper theme. The ear was literary but had substance.

In 'The Drive-In' the language is less formal, the detail of more importance. It is within touching distance, precise, tangible: 'The earth grinds to black butter under the tyres' is seeing almost nose-to-ground. The cultural references float in and float again and we are left with the loss of things slipping away with the film. That sense of slippage, cry and desire is key to Nick Makoha's work. It is the exile element.

There is another narrative in 'Father Cornelius', where verses of three lines hover between poetry and prose. I liked the sharpness of eye and ear in this, the short story material tipping into rhythm, underneath it the sure feeling for the corrupt and the chancy.

'Beatitude', the most recent of poems to be started, returns us to the domain of 'Prayers for exiled poets' but now it is less general, more specific, more direct. There is a distinct rhetorical pulse to the lines, which are long – the characteristic Makoha line is long and packs in a great deal – but move energetically. He discovers images such as the quilt of bristling static that muffle tears.

There is in Makoha's work an intriguing balance between the immediate and the stately that fits his material and offers possibilities for expansion and further exploration. All that – his personal history, the history of his country and the leaving of it – suggests to me a talent at the beginning of a genuinely important road. ■

The Drive-In

PLOT:

*The chessboard is the world, the pieces are the phenomena of the
Universe, the rules of the game are what we call the laws of Nature
and the player on the other side is hidden from us* – THOMAS HUXLEY

SCENE:

In the Datsun we follow Thika road to its natural end.
Where it curves, cars trail behind us in a wagon train.
The earth grinds to black butter under the tyres.

I am the voyeur trying to fit the images to the frame.
The name of the film is gone but Roger Moore is Bond.
A comet of light rays move towards the screen.

In this tail of celestial dust dragonflies float in the inertia.
My eyes obediently follow the credits,
a dark watermark of words against a canvas altar.

Outside the moon expands as rain drips off the trees.
Beyond the verandah a familiar sky hangs in the air.
These visions are a river of time and memory.

STORY:

At the drive-in uncle Mike hangs the speaker on the
        passenger's side window.
15 miles outside of Nairobi this open-air cinema screen is a
        door in the dark.
It glows like the Kenyan sunset that moments earlier
        disappeared into the night.

My cousin's eyes are fixed on the woman with braided hair
　　　in the next car,
her body bending, bouncing and grunting in the arms of a
　　　married man.
At this speed their bodies are water and flour folding into one.

His excitement nudges my shoulder and whispers a novel
　　　into my ear.
I am sipping a Fanta soda in a glass bottle. The car stinks of
　　　fried chicken
in breadcrumbs. Two pieces remain in the bucket on the
　　　front seat.

My Uncle wants me to keep the bottle. It's worth a shilling.
All this noise is a hiss. The Lotus Esprit is coming out of
　　　the water.
James Bond throws a fish to the floor. I was born in a fishing
　　　village.

THE MAGIC HOUR:
My eyes spend more time in front of a screen than sleeping.
I look at this landscape to dream. Something else is slipping
　　　away:
As the credits fall I learn to say goodbye to things I knew by
　　　heart.

Prayers for exiled poets

1

God, bent in time, repeats himself,
CÉSAR VALLEJO

How will you know me in the city I call home, in which I
am a guest?
You will not find me in the womb. My birth is a bruise healed.

This evening in the silence I rose from my humiliation.
With brittle nails and torn garments I fell to the floor palms
facing down.

Shame and disgrace weighed on my head, I did not know
where to put my eyes.
In forgetting you and my country, my transgressions are larger
than me.

When the guilt reached my heart I spoke to you!
I am one of those children of Ugandan progeny who fled.

Cloaked in night I left my kings and clans in captivity,
their blood and land at the mercy of the rifle.

Today foreign chiefs use our machetes
and lust for blood to rule us.

2

when you ask me where I have been
...I would have to tell how dirt mottles rocks.
How the river, running, runs out of itself.
PABLO NERUDA

Prayers no longer hold up these walls in my absence.
My own country rebukes me. I hold the world on my back.

Look for me in translation. In my own language you will go
      unanswered,
My Ugandan passports are a quiet place of ruin.

Where I come from money is water slipping through their
      hands.
They eat what falls from the trees and turn the flesh to gin.

I am of the same fruit and close to extinction.
My only root is my father's name. Both of us removed from
      the soil.

In recent times, despite my deeds you let me stay
No longer in bondage between earth and sky. No longer

do I hide in my own shadow. No longer waiting to stop
      waiting.
This rock becomes a sanctuary from which I can repair the
      ruins.

You have given me back my eyes.

Father Cornelius

With three torn hundred-dollar bills, he made the last table of six at the end of the second day. His seven-deuce offsuit in the big blind, flopped a full house, which he slow-played against a pair of aces and red kings. This hand eliminated the final two players for a seat in the finals at a bar.

Here's the dirt. They used to call him the Saint. Learnt to play poker close to the vest by watching Texas Slim and Johnny Ross, who won $10,000 at the Texas Amarillo Slim's tournament in the 80s. He never chased cards, and mumbled when the dealer tapped the table.

Saint mastered the bluff while training as a pastor in Nairobi "private" games for high stakes after confession. His wit and charm took their chips, harvesting the tells in their eyes and hands. After the river card he'd take you by the hand and pray, *Receive the Body and Blood of Christ.*

Father Cornelius offered wafers and a swig of Brugal to his travelling congregation. Always on his way to some place else, with a pack of playing cards tucked under the belt. Now middle-aged, his hairline receding like a low tide, his lips mouthing a number.

Beneath the soft lights of Nairobi Casino roulette tables spun like fans in the bayou. Past the cranked levers of fruit machines, rings of tobacco smoke left the corners of his mouth, right hand tweaked a pile of chips, dog collar in pocket as he eyed the waitress through black spectacles.

In cracked stilettos she poured him a Cuban Mojito in a tall glass. Two shots of dark rum topped up by the flask in his blazer. Sucking on the lemon he would swirl fistfuls of fresh mint leaves with his cigar. The flop was already on the table, if he bet now the pot would be too shallow.

After a minute stare he pushed his chips in the middle and ordered a plate of *nyama choma*. The crowd knew he needed the risk of looking at the river card. Under his lifted thumb the jack and nine of diamonds. After swigs of Brugal curses turned to prayers to a God of small things.

Beatitude

When a rebel leader promises you the world seen in commercials,
he will hold a shotgun to the radio announcer's mouth,
and use a quilt of bristling static to muffle the tears.

When the bodies disappear, discarded like the husk of mangoes.
He will weep with you in those hours of reckoning and
       judgement
into the hollow night when the crowds disperse.

When by paraffin light his whiskey breath tells you
your mother's wailings in your father's bed, are a song
for our nation and sits with you on the veranda to witness the
       sunrise,

say nothing. Slaughter your herd. Feed the soldiers
who looted your mills and factories. Let them dance
in your garden while an old man watches.

Then, when they sleep and your blood turns to kerosene,
find your mother gathering water at the well to stave off
the burning. Shave her head with a razor from the kiosk.

When the fury has gathered, take her hand and run
past the fields an odour of blood and bones. Past the checkpoint,
past the swamp to towards the smoky disc flaring in the horizon.

Run till your knuckles become as white as handkerchiefs,
run into the night's fluorescent silence, run till your lungs
become a furnace of flames. Run past the border.

Run till you no longer see yourself in other men's eyes.
Run past sleep, past darkness visible.
Stop when you find a country where they do not know your
 name.

JANET KOFI-TSEKPO

■ **JANET KOFI-TSEKPO** has had poetry and prose included in various international journals and anthologies, and is working towards her first collection. She currently runs a national professional development programme for the cultural sector, and lives in London. ■

■ MICHAEL SCHMIDT:

Anyone glancing at the shapes of Janet Kofi-Tsekpo's four poems in this anthology might assume that she is a conventional formalist. There is a sonnet, a poem in four tercets, a sestina, and a poem in two tight eight-line stanzas. There is a sense of great care about the poems, and of restraint. The more one looks, however, the more one is aware that the poems themselves are looking, and looking out. Their occasions may lie in literature (Eudora Welty, Rumi, Ashbery perhaps), the lenses may appear to be conventional, and yet what matters is not what lens you hold but what you see through it. Of these four poems the one that for me has the most authority is 'Eudora Welty' because the language works so well, is muscular without losing lyricism, is narrative without losing the broader properties of form. The one I most enjoy, and come back to time after time, is 'The Book of Puddle'.

These poems are exemplary, and they belong to the poet. But at the core of the mentoring relationship is, I hope, an enablement that these pieces, which have passed through workshops and many other filters, don't quite enjoy. 'The Book of Puddle' is the point of greatest promise here because the chosen form is an akimbo form; it forces the language and the language forces the content and things happen that are beyond the normal reach of the writer and her reader. The poem has a mind of its own. A mentoring relationship may allow the poet to write – yes – more loosely, with greater freedom: she knows what she has done: but what can she do? She does not want to jump up and down on the same spot.

I am excited when I read these four poems. But my commitment to Janet's work is based on the sequences which she is composing, slowly, at a pace I want to protect. Poetry of the kind she writes is not subjectable to deadlines. She is taking narrative in unusual directions and her compression of metaphor and incident seem to be breaking new formal and thematic ground. She is finding her way and her reader follows her, adopting her pace, travelling 'under a bright star' and hearing her begin to speak 'a new language'. ■

Eudora Welty

FROM *Death of a Traveling Salesman*

To this end of nowhere! And yet he'd come
with what seemed a vital sense of purpose,
his face as soft and sturdy as a mule's,
the back-breaking weight of his body
heaving him out of his car to the door.
The man and his wife stood together
as if they'd been placed there like wooden toys.
He sat in a chair and watched as they chopped
logs and made a fire, almost content.
Only, something else stirred in the corner
of the room, a wild rude thing like a turkey's
head, too small to be a child's but making
little breathing sounds, thin and reedy like
a tune from a pipe. It was this that broke him.

Poem for Rumi

You're indecent, innocent animal
leaking all over my edges. You breathe
gently like a sleeping infant.

Another second, and you'll be your own
patter of feet in the distance, a quiet
child's cold-hearted daydream. Remember

the maggot I told you about, the one
that wriggled away as I chased it by the bins,
bleach sinking into its flesh like burning

milk. It moved persistently, as we do,
by the same invisible thread that ties me
like a shoelace, like a prank, to you.

Rose Garden, Lidice

These roses will unfold like women's thighs
one unexpected morning before Sabbath.
Their sweet blood smell will take down every man;
a field of assassins. After the men
came mothers, grandmothers, and then the children
were taken. The landscape makes delicate
adjustments. This rose is a bullet,
an effusion of gases. After the war,

we women came back from the camps
to the silent village. We had to make new,
marrying the men from over the border
who rebuilt our homes. Our second round
of children fight over the same patch. Life
is life, they say, and death, death; but look,
the earth is inflamed with our roses,
their fresh petals scattered regardless.

The Book of Puddle

Listen to the rain, as we settle down
into bed, falling into a puddle
on the kerb, filling up the night under
a lamplight, as if we were in marshland
or the dark oasis of a desert.
As if it was the hidden language

of nomads, a whole other language
entirely, the rain keeps beating down
on the tarmac, the road like a desert
splashed with libations. But soon the puddle
has spread, turning the landscape into marshland,
and everything we've known is now under

water, until even the moon falls under
the sky as the rain's persistent language
stuns the stars into silence. Now marshland
is the new territory, and written down
with each raindrop is the Book of Puddle,
forbidding the old ways of the desert

and the nomads who live in the desert
to live there or live anywhere as, under
new laws commonly known as the Puddle
Laws, they no longer speak the right language.
The nomads protest but are beaten down
by harsh rains that cut through the marshlands.

It's difficult to live in the marshlands,
but there is no longer any desert
that isn't already claimed by rain, down
to the last grain of sand found once under
a stone, which soon disappeared. The language
of nomads is hidden in a puddle.

Now all must observe the Book of Puddle
and live by the Puddle Laws in the marshlands.
Rain must fall; we must speak a new language.
No one can think of those from the desert.
Through no fault but their own, they lie under
the water. The rains keep beating them down.

Some of them dream that a lone puddle down
in the heart of the marshlands speaks, under
a bright star, the language of the desert.

■ BIOGRAPHIES OF EDITORS:

Bernardine Evaristo's books include *Hello Mum*, a novella about teenage knife crime (Penguin, 2010); *Lara*, a verse novel based on her family history spanning England, Nigeria, Ireland, Germany and Brazil (Bloodaxe Books, 2009); *Blonde Roots*, a satirical prose novel in which Africans enslave Europeans (Penguin, 2008); *Soul Tourists*, a novel-with-verse, which explores Europe's black history (Penguin, 2005); *The Emperor's Babe*, a verse novel set in 300 AD (Penguin, 2001). She edited the Granta anthology *NW15* (New Writing 15) in 2007 with novelist Maggie Gee. She has written for theatre and BBC radio and her reviews appear in the *Guardian, Independent, Times* and *Financial Times* newspapers. Her awards include the Orange Prize Youth Panel Award, Big Red Read Award, EMMA Best Book Award, a NESTA Fellowship Award and an Arts Council Writers Award. Her books have been a Book of the Year nine times in British newspapers and *The Emperor's Babe* was a *Times* '100 Best Books of the Decade' title in 2009. She is a Fellow of the Royal Society of Literature and of the Royal Society of Arts, and she was awarded an MBE for services to literature in 2009. Website: www.bevaristo.net

Daljit Nagra comes from a Punjabi background. He was born and raised in London then Sheffield. He has won several prestigious prizes for his poetry. In 2004, he won the Forward Prize for Best Individual Poem with 'Look We Have Coming to Dover!' This was also the title of his first collection, published by Faber & Faber in 2007. This won the Forward Prize for Best First Collection and The South Bank Show Decibel Award. His second collection, *Tippoo Sultan's Incredible White-Man Eating Tiger-Toy Machine!!!*, is due from Faber in 2011.

■ BIOGRAPHIES OF MENTORS:

Paul Farley, born in Liverpool and now living in Lancaster, is the author of three poetry collections. *The Boy from the Chemist Is Here to See You* was awarded a Forward Prize and a Somerset Maugham Award in 1998. *The Ice Age* was a Poetry Book Society Choice and won the 2002 Whitbread Poetry Award and *Tramp in Flames* was shortlisted for the International Griffin Prize in 2006. He was the 1999 *Sunday Times* Young Writer of the Year. A poet, essayist and critic, he also writes drama and documentary features for BBC Radio. In 2009 he received an RSL Jerwood Award for Non-Fiction and the E.M. Forster Award from the American Academy of Arts and Letters. His forthcoming book of non-fiction, *Edgelands: Journeys into England's Last Wilderness* (2010), written with Michael Symmons Roberts, won the 2009 Jerwood Prize for Non-Fiction. He is currently working on *The Electric Poly-Olbion*, due in 2012.

W.N. Herbert was born in Dundee in 1961, and educated there and at Oxford, where he published his thesis on Hugh MacDiarmid (*To Circumjack MacDiarmid*, OUP, 1992). He has published seven volumes of poetry and five pamphlets, and he is widely anthologised. After several residencies in Scotland, he moved to Newcastle in 1994 to take up the Northern Arts Literary Fellowship and has remained there ever since, holding residencies with Cumbria Arts in Education and the Wordsworth Trust. He taught in the Department of Creative Writing at Lancaster University (1996-2002), and is now Professor of Poetry and Creative Writing in the School of English at Newcastle University. His most recent collection, *Bad Shaman Blues* (Bloodaxe Books, 2006), was a Poetry Book Society Recommendation, and was shortlisted for the Saltire Award and the T.S. Eliot Prize. He is currently co-editing *Jade Ladder*, an anthology of contemporary Chinese poetry.

Mimi Khalvati has published six collections with Carcanet Press, including *Selected Poems* (2000) and *The Chine* (2002). She is the founder of The Poetry School, where she teaches, and was the Coordinator from 1997 to 2004. She is also co-editor of the Poetry School's three anthologies of new writing published by Enitharmon Press, including *I am twenty people!* (2007), co-edited with Stephen Knight. Her most recent collection, *The Meanest Flower* (Carcanet, 2007), was a Poetry Book Society Recommendation, a *Financial Times* Book of the Year and was shortlisted for the T.S. Eliot Prize. In 2006, she received a Cholmondeley Award from the Society of Authors and is a Fellow of the Royal Society of Literature.

Stephen Knight was born in Swansea. He has been a creative writing tutor for 25 years and, in that capacity, currently works for the University of Glamorgan, City Lit, and Goldsmiths, University of London. He has reviewed poetry and fiction for *London Magazine*, *Poetry Wales*, the *TLS* and *The Independent on Sunday*. His books of poetry are *Flowering Limbs* (1993), a Poetry Book Society Choice, *The Sandfields Baudelaire* (1996), *Dream City Cinema* (1996) and, for children, *Sardines and Other Poems* (2004). He received a Gregory Award in 1987, won the 1992 National Poetry Competition, and his novel, *Mr Schnitzel*, was the Arts Council of Wales Book of the Year in 2001.

Pascale Petit's latest book is *What the Water Gave Me – Poems after Frida Kahlo* (Seren, 2010). She has published five poetry collections, including two shortlisted for the T.S. Eliot Prize and which were books of the year in the *Times Literary Supplement* and *Independent*. A bilingual edition of *The Zoo Father* is published in Mexico and a poem from the book was shortlisted for a Forward Prize. She co-edited *Tying the Song*, the first anthology from The Poetry School (Enitharmon, 2000). In 2004 the Poetry Book Society selected her as one of its Next Generation Poets. She has won numerous awards, including three from Arts Council England. Petit trained as a sculptor at the Royal College of Art. She has worked as Poetry Editor for *Poetry London* and was the Royal Literary Fund Fellow at Middlesex University, 2007-09. She currently teaches poetry courses at Tate Modern. Website: www.pascalepetit.co.uk. Blog: pascalepetit.blogspot.com

Michael Schmidt was born in Mexico in 1947. He studied at Harvard and at Wadham College, Oxford. He is currently Professor of Poetry at Glasgow University, where he is convenor of the creative writing programme. He is a founder (1969) and editorial and managing director of Carcanet Press Limited, and a founder (1972) and general editor of *PN Review*. A Fellow of the Royal Society of Literature, he received an OBE in 2006 for services to poetry.

Michael Symmons Roberts's fifth book of poems, *The Half-Healed*, was published by Cape in 2008. His poetry has won the Whitbread Poetry Award, and been shortlisted for the Griffin International Poetry Prize, the Forward Prize, and twice for the T.S. Eliot Prize. He has received major awards from the Arts Council and the Society of Authors. As a librettist, his continuing collaboration with composer James MacMillan has led to two BBC Proms choral commissions, song cycles, music theatre works and an opera for the Welsh National Opera, *The Sacrifice*, which won the RPS Award for opera. His broadcast work includes, *A Fearful Symmetry*, for Radio 4 – which won the Sandford St Martin Prize, and *Last Words*, commissioned by Radio 4 to mark the first anniversary of 9/11. He has also published two novels, and is Professor of Poetry at Manchester Metropolitan University. Website: www.symmonsroberts.com

Catherine Smith's first short poetry collection, *The New Bride* (Smith/Doorstop) was shortlisted for the Forward Prize for Best First Collection, 2001. Her first full-length collection, *The Butcher's Hands* (Smith/Doorstop) was a Poetry Book Society Recommendation and was shortlisted for the Aldeburgh/Jerwood Prize, 2004. In 2004 she was voted one of *Mslexia*'s 'Top Ten UK Women Poets' and was included in the Poetry Book Society's Next Generation Poets promotion. Her latest collection, *Lip* (Smith/Doorstop), was shortlisted for the Forward Prize for Best Collection, 2008. She also writes short fiction and radio drama and teaches for Sussex University, Varndean College in Brighton, the University of Sussex and the Arvon Foundation. Her first short fiction collection is due out next year, She has adapted three of her short stories for a stage performance. She is working on her next poetry collection and a novel.

John Stammers is an award-winning poet and editor. His first collection, *Panoramic Lounge-bar* (Picador, 2001) won the Forward Prize for Best First Collection. His second collection, *Stolen Love Behaviour* (Picador, 2005), was a Poetry Book Society Choice and shortlisted for the T.S. Eliot Prize and Forward Prize. His third collection, *Interior Night* (Picador), is published in 2010. He is a former editor of *Magma* poetry magazine. He is currently editing a selected Gerard Manley Hopkins for Faber and Faber. He has taught widely, including at Cambridge University where he was Judith E. Wilson Fellow. He is editor of the academic journal *British and Irish Contemporary Poetry*.

George Szirtes has published some fourteen books of poetry, his first, *The Slant Door*, being awarded the Geoffrey Faber Memorial Prize in 1979. He has also translated a great many books of poetry and fiction from the Hungarian, as well as editing various anthologies. His collection, *Reel*, was awarded the 2004 T.S. Eliot Prize, his *New and Collected Poems* was published in 2008, and *The Burning of the Books and Other Poems* (2009) was shortlisted for the 2009 T.S. Eliot Prize, all three titles from Bloodaxe. He became a Fellow of the Royal Society of Literature in 1982. His Newcastle/Bloodaxe Poetry Lectures, *Fortinbras at the Fishhouses*, was published in 2010. He teaches at the University of East Anglia. He was born in Hungary and came to England as a refugee following the 1956 Uprising. He lives in Norfolk with his artist wife, Clarissa Upchurch.

ACKNOWLEDGEMENTS

Many people have contributed their time, energy and good-will towards making this anthology possible, as well as to the *Free Verse* report and The Complete Works mentoring project that followed it. These are: Arts Council England's Literature Department, especially its Literature Officers Kate Griffin and Gemma Seltzer; Spread the Word Literature Development Agency, especially Director Emma Hewett and Project Manager Nathalie Teitler; journalist Danuta Kean and consultant Melanie Larsen who produced the *Free Verse* report; Bloodaxe Books, especially editor Neil Astley; the original advisory committee for all three stages of this project: Patience Agbabi, Moniza Alvi, Ruth Borthwick, Fiona Sampson and Matthew Hollis alongside Bernardine Evaristo and Daljit Nagra; all the poets' mentors on The Complete Works: Paul Farley, W.N. Herbert, Mimi Khalvati, Stephen Knight, Pascale Petit, Michael Schmidt, Michael Symmons Roberts, Catherine Smith, John Stammers and George Szirtes; and Chris Ofili for his kind permission to use one of his paintings on our cover, and to Kathy Stephenson and Victoria Miro Gallery for their help.

Thanks also to the photographers: Naomi Woddis (Karen McCarthy Woolf, Rowyda Amin and Denise Saul), Matthew Joyce (Mir Mahfuz Ali), Nicola Griffiths (Roger Robinson), Ania Tomaszeska-Nelson (Shazea Quraishi), Lyndon Douglas courtesy of renaissance one (Malika Booker), T. Chan-Sam (Seni Seneviratne), Johnny Munday (Nick Makoha), Dabinder Rai (Janet Kofi-Tsekpo), Katie Vandyck (Bernardine Evaristo), Sarah Lee (Daljit Nagra).

PREVIOUS PUBLICATIONS

Malika Booker: none of the poems included here have been previously published.

Mir Mafhuz Ali: none of the poems included here have been previously published.

Rowyda Amin: 'Frost Fair' and 'Monkey Daughter', *Magma* 45, 2009; 'Mojave', *Notes From the Underground*, Issue 3, March 2009; 'Insect Studies', *The Shuffle Anthology 2008-2009* (The Shuffle Press, November 2009).

Karen McCarthy Woolf: none of the poems included have been previously published.

Nick Makoha: none of the poems included have been previously published.

Seni Seneviratne: previous version of 'Sitting for the Mistress' was published in *Creative Freedom* (Peepal Tree Press, 2008).

Denise Saul: none of the poems included have been previously published.

Jan Kofi Tsekpo: none of the poems included have been previously published.

Shazea Quraishi: poems previously published in *Modern Poetry in Translation*, 2009.

Roger Robinson: poems taken from collection *Suckle* (flipped eye, 2009).

■ ABOUT SPREAD THE WORD

Spread the Word is London's leading writer development agency.

It is a catalyst for developing writers with a strong reputation for providing bold, playful and accessible support for writers of all levels. From networking events to publisher and agent talks, advice surgeries to an online city of shared stories, the organisation takes a collaborative approach to developing writers ensuring that both they and the communities in which they live benefit from the work carried out.

For more than 15 years, Spread the Word has been working in partnership with arts organisations, bookshops, libraries, local authorities, schools and community groups. Services, projects, programmes and consultancy models include:

- Creative writing workshops and writers' residencies
- Programming including author events, talks, workshops and showcases
- Participative digital media events
- Access to publishers and agents
- Careers services for writers including events, advice and information for beginners and specialised career professional development for advanced writers including mentoring
- Database of professional CRB checked writers
- Education programmes
- Publishing

Spread the Word provides key employment opportunities for writers, offers skills development and training, contributes to the growth of literacy, promotes wellbeing and social cohesion.

www.spreadtheword.org.uk <http://www.spreadtheword.org.uk>